Cookbook for Getting Your Kid to College

Also by Kira Janene Holt
Rapid Descent: Nightmare in the Grand Canyon

WHAT THE EXPERTS ARE SAYING

"This is **a very thorough and comprehensive aid** for helping students and parents to navigate the college going process. This is all done in an easy to understand manner with step-by-step pointers. This guide provides an extensive list of websites that students and parents can explore to customize the college search. I appreciate the pros and cons noted for the common pitfalls that are out there to take advantage of the unsuspecting parent and student attempting to find the right college and even more so for finding financial aid. With this guide in hand, students should be able to explore successfully the road to success for finding the right college, and parents should be able to offer the necessary support for their child navigating the ever allusive process without giving up or taking over the responsibility. A wonderful guide for every family to use as a reference and to pick up periodically to see they are still on the right track. This should be in the hands of all parents who aspire for their children attending college."

Carolyn A. Greer, EDD
Former Director of Counseling and Guidance
for two large school districts in Texas

"The *Cookbook...* is **what every parent with a college age kid needs to read and know**. You'll learn about the many education options available from university to trade programs. What the ACT and SAT are and the differences. Plus learn about the admissions process, financial aid and dozens of additional resources."

James Jacobs, Chief Operating Officer
Texas Counseling Association

Cookbook for Getting Your Kid to College

The College Dream Dinner: Planning, Readiness, Admission

KIRA JANENE HOLT

Kiowa Hill Publishing, LLC
Winberly, TX

Cookbook for Getting Your Kid to College
Copyright ©2012 Kira Janene Holt
All Rights Reserved

No portion of this book may be copied, reproduced, or transmitted in any form or by any means, electronic or otherwise, including recording, photocopying, or inclusion in any information storage and retrieval system, without the express written permission of the publisher and author, except for brief excerpts quoted in published reviews.

First Edition
Printed in the United States

Kiowa Hill Publishing, LLC

Publisher's Cataloging-in-Publication Data

Holt, Kira Janene.
  Cookbook for getting your kid to college : a guide for helping your kid navigate the road to college / Kira Janene Holt.
     p. cm.
    ISBN: 978-1-937989-03-3 (pbk.)
    ISBN: 978-1-937989-02-6 (e-book: EPUB)
    1. Universities and colleges—United States—Admission. 2. College choice—United States. 3. Student aid—United States. 4. College applications—United States.   I. Title.
LB2351.2 .H65 2012
378.1`61—dc23
                                   2012910032

My parents, Donald B. Holt and Norma Jean Lynch Holt, always stressed the importance of education even when I didn't take it seriously. I never knew I had the choice not to go to college. This manual is dedicated to them and to the millions of other parents who want to help their children make the best possible choices for their future.

It is also dedicated to the unsung heroes in our nation's schools—the teachers, professional school counselors, and administrators who work tirelessly long hours to educate our collective children. I am in constant awe of their dedication and passion for education.

Contents

1 Introduction
Setting the College Readiness Table

7 Is Your Kid Hungry? Education Does Pay!
College Graduation Is the Main Course that Keeps Pantries Fuller and Continues to Nourish over a Lifetimev

13 Know Your Ingredients
Colleges Come in a Variety of Flavors

15 Key Ingredients
The Different Types of Colleges and Universities

21 Searching Out the Perfect Ingredients For Your Kid's College Meal
What Does He Want for Dinner?

27 College Entrance Exams

35 Finished Shopping and Sampling Hors D'oeuvres?
It's Time to Select the Main Course: Narrowing the College Choice

41 Kitchen Time: Preparing the Kitchen Makes Cooking the Main Course Easier
Your Kid and College Entrance Exams

55 Picking Out a Choice Cut of Meat
Applying to College

57 How Long Does the Meat Need to Marinade?
Admission Acceptance Plans

61 Combining All the Ingredients
Pulling the Meal Together

College Applications

71 Paying for the Meal
Finding Money for Your Kid's College

85 Finding Help to Pay for the Meal
Scholarship Money for Your Kid's College

93 Resource Links

97 Relax and Enjoy the Meal

101 Quick List of Guide Web sites

About the Author

Introduction
Setting the College Readiness Table

You want your kid to go to college. I applaud the desire. Every parent wants her child to succeed, do well, and start the path to adulthood with one foot forward. My first question is does your child want to go to college as much as you want him/her to go? The reason I ask is there is much involved in preparing for college. Your child needs to lead this process instead of you doing it for him, and this cookbook will help you clarify the steps he must take to ensure he makes the best choices.

Okay, I want you to understand that I'm going to use "her" for the parent and "him" for the student. I want to be helpful, not formal in writing. Mothers often take a lead role in helping students prepare for college, and to be clear I'll use "him" as the student.

There are many choices when it comes to postsecondary education. Each path has advantages as well as shortcomings so it is important to consider why one school choice or financial aid decision may win over another. I started college because, frankly, I didn't know I had a choice. My parents had always told my brother and me that we would go to college. My mother went to a university and then graduated from a business college. My father went to college on the GI Bill after the Korean War. He graduated from Tulsa University with a degree in petroleum engineering. I firmly believe setting the expectations early that your kid will go to college will go a long way in him taking this process seriously. I also believe there is more to college readiness than setting the expectations and will address that when I talk about career exploration.

I was never the poster child for college readiness even though my folks set the expectations. I didn't know what I wanted to do with my life, nor did I really know the questions to ask about career exploration and how careers tie into college majors. I was sixteen when I graduated from high school. I turned seventeen a few weeks later, but remained immature long into my twenties. I didn't graduate early because I was a strong, academic contender, but because I was bored. I was smart enough, but had heard "she doesn't apply herself" at too many parent conferences to count.

I didn't like high school, didn't feel like I fit in. To be honest, I was an aspiring "hippy" with conservative parents who had big expectations for their children. I looked at the credits I needed to graduate from high school and found that with taking senior English and government during the summer after my junior year, I could leave high school in the dust, jump into adulthood, and hang with a new group. So why am I sharing my story? I'm not some elitist with a plan that had been laid out since before I was born.

I'm part of the masses. I've worked all my adult life in education and specifically helping students make the transition from high school to college. Even though my parents set the college expectation, I didn't have a clear direction of what I wanted to do. Does this sound familiar?

College has become a huge financial investment for parents and children. I believe that if you and your kid plan to spend serious cash (and time) investing in the future, it's best to make the most informed decisions possible. This cookbook is intended to serve as an inexpensive roadmap to help understand to choices and paths to college.

Sometimes my opinions leak out. I'll try to label them if I catch myself. You cannot work in this field for as long as I have without developing some opinions.

Cookbook for Getting Your Kid to College

Just so you know who I am, let me tell you a bit more about me. I have a bachelor's degree in English. My master's degree is in Human Services with an emphasis on psychological and social services. I returned to school for a master of fine arts in creative writing. I'm not sure if it's the right path, but I have written several novels and want to improve my writing skills.

I taught middle school and high school English. I've worked for two universities (one private and one public) helping students make the transition from high school to college. For the last sixteen years, I've worked for an educational publisher. Every year, I speak to thousands of school people on college readiness issues.

While a college education doesn't guarantee an easy career path, I believe with my whole heart that it will help all students achieve a brighter future as compared to those students without any college. I see through my work that many kids have wonderful goals beyond college. The job of this manual is to help you to help your kid enter college as prepared as possible and ready to achieve his goals.

Let us get started helping your kid make that leap from high school to college. My promise is to make this cookbook as straightforward as possible. I know you have a full life and many responsibilities.

I would suggest you skim through this entire guide so that you know what is ahead in the full meal deal of making the transition from high school to college. There are many ingredients necessary to make the college table nourishing and enjoyable. I hope you bought this earlier in your kid's high school career rather than later. If your kid is already a senior, he's going to have to start cooking harder and faster than if he had started down the college path in grade 10 or 11.

Is Your Kid Hungry? Education Does Pay!

College Graduation Is the Main Course that Keeps Pantries Fuller and Continues to Nourish over a Lifetimev

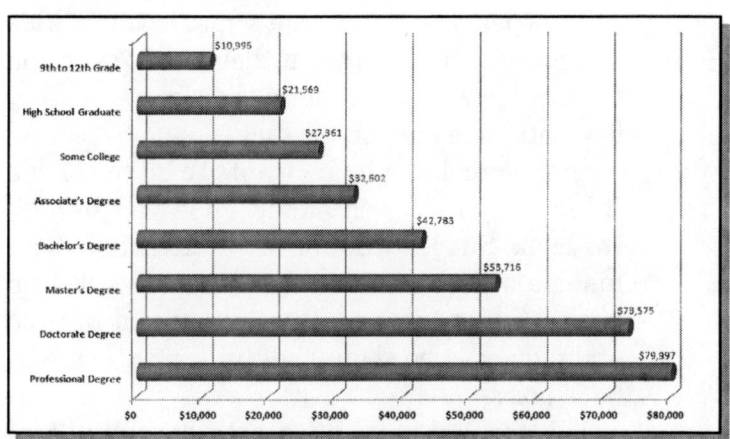

Source: U.S. Census Bureau American Community Survey 2006-2008

Cookbook for Getting Your Kid to College

The more education your kid receives, the better shot he has at surviving downturns in the workplace, but of course there are no guarantees. In the chart above, median annual income means that half the people make above that amount and half below that amount.

It's important for your kid to consider why he wants to go to college. Is it to learn skills for a job? Have you always set college expectations in front of him and he doesn't know he has a choice? Are all his friends going to college? Does he have a burning passion to a specific career pathway and college is the route?

Personally, my favorite is learning how to think more critically. I believe college is a place to open up to new ideas, new people, and new ways of looking at the world. I'm a strong advocate for liberal arts education—to learn for the sake of learning, but that's me. Today's kids are going to have reinvent themselves over and over as they move through their careers. Very few will have one job for life.

Ask your kid why he wants to go to college. If his reply is, "I don't know," don't let him off the hook. Suggest that he begin thinking about his goals and tell him that you will ask him again. College is a serious investment of time and money so he should be thinking about why he is going.

This would also be a great time to tell him you're on his college readiness team and that you're both in the kitchen together. He is the head chef while you are the sous-chef (the second chef in command). There may be other people in the kitchen helping, but as sous-chef, your job is to be his primary support system.

Your kid doesn't have to know the answer to why he wants to go to college today. It's a good idea to plant the seed that specific college majors are tied to careers. If there is a career out in the world that excites him, he's much more likely to be successful in college as he works toward his goal.

The majority of high schools and colleges have access to an interest inventory in the counseling office or career center. An interest inventory asks your kid a series of questions about activities he would like or not like to do. Have your kid take one! Contact the career center or your kid's professional school counselor for information. Why, you ask? We want young people to make a connection between their interests and careers.

There are over 12,000 occupations out in the world today. Some jobs become obsolete and fade out of existence while developing technology creates new jobs that I couldn't have imagined thirty years ago.

How many jobs can you name? Let's say you can name 1,000. That's generous. I'd be hard pressed to name 1,000 occupations. You are likely going to start with occupations that your friends and family members have, the jobs in your area, and the jobs you see in popular media. So will your kid. Remember there are another 11,000 jobs you don't know about. Your kid needs to explore the world of work and the possibilities out there so that he can start to see the link between what his interests are and what kinds of jobs relate to his interests.

We may even want to take his interests one-step further. Let's ask the question of how does your kid's interests measure against his abilities? I see so many young people wanting to go into forensic sciences, health care, and business but fail to enroll in rigorous math and science classes in high school. Great aspirations! I want your kid to understand that the classes he takes in high school have a direct impact on how difficult his college classes seem. Additionally, if your kid is interested in a career area that doesn't mesh with his academic abilities, the earlier you and he find this out, the more time he will have in high school to develop those abilities.

If your kid takes ACT's college readiness assessments (EXPLORE or PLAN) in grade eight, nine, or ten, your kid has taken an interest inventory as well as an assessment of his English, math, reading and science skills. Many states and school systems pay for these assessments so ask if you don't know if your kid has taken it.

You and your kid can visit ACT's World of Work Map at

www.ExploreStudent.org
www.PlanStudent.org

College career centers and high school guidance departments are the best place to start investigating careers, interests, and college majors. Your kid's professional high school counselor as well as a college career center will be your greatest allies in making the right choices. This might be a great time for you and your kid to meet his school counselor if you haven't already.

The ACT college entrance exam also includes an interest inventory so if your kid has taken the ACT, he already has a completed interest inventory readily available. He can use that interest inventory to make the connection between college majors and career. If he has taken the ACT he can go to this link, http://www.ACTstudent.org/wwm/, and see how occupations relate to interests.

Safe sites that provide great career information

http://www.bls.gov/ooh/about/sources-of-career-information.htm
U.S Department of Labor, Bureau of Labor Statistics.

The Occupational Outlook Handbook—online. This government site updates occupations every two years. Extensive listing of different occupations by a variety of search tactics. Available in English and Spanish.

```
http://www.CareerOneStop.org/Explore
Careers/SelfAssessments
/FindAssessments.aspx
```
Assessment of interests and abilities. CareerOneStop is sponsored by the U.S. Department of Labor, Employment and Training Administration.

Know Your Ingredients
Colleges Come in a Variety of Flavors

Hundreds of schools out there could want your kid to attend their school, and each college brings a unique flavor and personality to the table. It's like grocery shopping for the life table your kid will set. I usually shop the same stores because I know where everything is located and I'm comfortable there. When I step into a new grocery store, I assess the feel and layout of the store and notice if the prices are higher or lower than my usual stores. I want to see if they carry my favorite brands.

Colleges and universities are similar to grocery stores. Each one has a different feel, cost, and landscape from every other school, even if they exist in the same town. One may have been built in the 1800s and have the buildings' towers jutting up in gothic spires. There are students studying under shady oak trees and massive lawns in front of ivy walls. Two miles down the street is a modern campus with students who commute to area apartments instead of living in traditional dorms. Nowadays there are even schools housed in what used to be big box stores. Every school is just as unique as your kid is. The trick is finding a college that best matches what your kid (and to some extent you) wants. So let's get general about the types of college and universities from which your kid can choose.

Universities typically provide students access to a bachelor's degree. That is a degree that may average four or five years, depending on the program of study. They may also provide master and doctoral degrees. They may have a focus on research and larger class sizes. Colleges may provide associate, bachelor, and master degrees, depending on the institution. There are even colleges within a university, for example The College of Natural Sciences within XYZ University.

Many schools that used to be XYZ College changed their name to XYZ University so don't be stumped by a name. The school where I received my bachelor's degree is now Texas State University. When I graduated, it was Southwest Texas State University. Previously, the university part had instead been college, teacher's college, and before that it was known as a normal school (that's where teachers went).

Key Ingredients
The Different Types of Colleges and Universities

Private Colleges and Universities
Neither state nor federal governments run these schools and they can be associated with religious institutions. For example, the Brothers of the Holy Cross of the Catholic Church founded Notre Dame while Baylor University is of Baptist church origin. While these schools often work from a mission, they generally do not limit their enrollment to students of their religion. That said there are a few private schools steeped in the traditions of their particular religious denomination and may require their students to attend church.

They may be evangelical and will let you know their religious requirements.

Private colleges and universities can be paid for with federal financial aid. Many are well endowed, which means someone or some foundation gave them money to help pay for students to go there. Many private schools receive federal grant monies targeted for research. Private colleges and universities are typically the most expensive to attend. They tend toward smaller class sizes and provide individual student attention.

Public Colleges or Universities

These schools receive money from the state and often the federal government. The governmental monies help cover the cost of student tuition, so these schools cost less than private ones. Since these schools receive money from their state government, they reserve the lowest tuition rates for students who reside within their state. It's called in-state tuition. Parents of traditional students (ages eighteen to twenty-four) must reside in the state for the student to claim in-state tuition. Some schools require that a parent have a residency of a year or more to claim in-state tuition. These colleges and universities often have the state's name in the school. Examples are University of Oklahoma and Iowa State University. These schools usually have larger class sizes than private schools. Some schools, especially those close to state borders, may grant in-state tuition rates to students who live on the other side of the state line.

Community Colleges, Junior Colleges, City Colleges

These schools tend to be local and grant associate degrees (two-year degrees). Many offer certificate programs, which are non-degree studies that teach specific job skills that enable a student to enter the workplace fast.

For example, my niece received a dental assistant certificate from a community college. After a few years of working as a dental assistant, she returned to the same college for an associate degree (two-year degree, although it really takes three years) in dental hygiene. She can work part-time as a dental assistant while returning for her associate degree. In Texas, where I live, certificate programs typically are tied to community colleges while other states may offer certificate programs at vocational/technical schools.

These community-based colleges typically receive monies from city and county government. Like public colleges, they offer the lowest tuition rates to the students who live within their borders. They tend to offer a wide variety of classes, in the evening as well as during the day. In addition to general classes such as English, math, history, and foreign languages, they also offer courses specific to the occupations in the community.

Vo-Tech Institutes and Technical Colleges

These vary from state to state. They started out offering technical training programs, but now also offer certificates, and many also have associate degree programs.

Commercial, For-Profit Institutions

This type of school's primary goal is to earn a profit for those who own the institution while also providing education. These are schools often advertising on television in the middle of the afternoon. They may offer anything from certificate programs all the way up to doctoral degrees, but the commercials on television target certificate and associate degrees. They are expensive and usually compete with what community colleges and technical schools will offer at a lower price.

Here's where I tell you what I think. Stay away from these schools! I think they're rip-offs. I've heard too many horror stories from people who thought they didn't have to pay anything and wound up defaulting on student loans they didn't even know they had. They faced huge financial aid messes when I counseled them about returning to school. If you're considering one of these schools, see if the community college or technical school has something similar. If you call or visit a for-profit college and they offer you everything you need to make your world perfect and it won't cost anything, run away. I'm not the only person who believes this. A Google search will reveal many links to funding controversies concerning these schools. Visit:

http://studentaid.ed.gov/students
/attachments/siteresources
/ChooseSchoolCarefully.pdf

Moreover, check out a recent Better Business Bureau article:

http://www.bbb.org/us/article/look-for
-seven-red-flags-when-applying-to-a-for
-profit-college-24540

Ivy League Schools

I'm not writing this guide to help you and your kid navigate the nation's most competitive colleges, but the information I put forth in this guide will help with applying there too. If the most competitive schools are your kid's dream, there are hundreds of books targeted toward perfecting personal interviews, writing the perfect admission essay, and gaining the competitive edge. I don't have anything against these schools. They're great and the written guides can help with admission. I'm writing this guide for the millions of parents and kids who want to find the other colleges and universities in the United States that can fit their needs.

You've heard the names: Harvard, Yale, Princeton, Wellesley, Vanderbilt, and Brown. I

Cookbook for Getting Your Kid to College

could go on and on, but the point I wanted to make is there are plenty of great schools, public and private, out there. What is important is regardless of the school's name, you need to help your kid navigate the transition from high school to college and find the school that is the best fit for him.

Searching Out the Perfect Ingredients For Your Kid's College Meal
What Does He Want for Dinner?

This section is a tale of 'do as I say, not as I did.' I attended four colleges during my undergraduate career. I didn't search out the right fit; I was more like a leaf blowing in the wind. I snacked from a variety of tables until I ended up with a full meal (degree).

I already wrote that I graduated from high school at sixteen. Back in the day, dorms didn't allow anyone under eighteen to live there with such limited supervision, and most schools required students to live on campus the first year. Combined with receiving my high school diploma in mid-August, I didn't have time to decide where I wanted to go. I headed to the closest junior college, Del Mar in Corpus Christi, Texas. After the first semester, my father transferred from Corpus to Denver. Still a minor, I transferred to a community college there. Six months later, Daddy received a promotion and we moved from Denver to Oklahoma City. I enrolled at the University of Oklahoma.

After a full year in Oklahoma, my father transferred back to Corpus (that's the oil business for you). Attending OU when they won a national championship, I knew I would never attend the University of Texas. I had heard rumors about a college named Southwest Texas State University. The school ranked nationally on the party circuit, and kids who had a hard time academically at Del Mar flourished at SWTSU. Decision made and off I went.

Remember, I had no clue as to why I was in college other than my parents told me that was where I needed to be. I'm not blaming them. I never had any career education or information shared with me when I was in high school. It's more I didn't have focus or direction. I had a vague idea about writing, but no idea what it entailed. My father suggested I become a geologist. I collected rocks so this worked too.

I share my story because it's a prime example of how not to make college choice decisions. I lost close to a full year of credits with all the transfers. I also lost credits changing my major from geology to English. As much as I hate to admit it, I also lost credits because I had no direction and spent lots of time goofing off. While I think setting those college expectations is important, combining the message with career exploration (and college majors that lead to those careers) will help your kid in not making the mistakes I did.

So how should your kid start searching colleges? The Internet is the best place to begin collecting information; call it surfing for schools. He can find unlimited information without leaving the house or his high school. Most colleges have developed extensive Web sites with their admission's department to inform potential students of their requirements and all the advantages their school can offer.

I suggest that your kid start some sort of data information management system. It doesn't have to be on the computer. Include columns for location, cost, admission criteria, application requirements, admission test requirements, and application and financial aid deadlines. He can start by jotting down information about the colleges he likes in a notebook. Consider this notebook a wish list of schools. If you have younger kids, they can also start their college wish list.

The sophomore and junior years are the best time to shop for colleges. If your kid is a senior, the time between wishing and applying may only be a few weeks. I love this activity for middle school students. It helps set the college readiness expectation as well as lets younger kids know that everything they do in high school has a direct influence on the acceptance to college.

One limitation of the Internet is that your kid will need to know a school's name to begin searching. Your kid can also search for colleges by key words (such as major), and there are a number of college search engines to help. The Web sites listed below are a great place to start.

www.collegenet.com
ACT's Web site

https://bigfuture.collegeboard.org/
SAT is delivered by the College Board. This site has planning information for parents, career information, and a section to help students organize their search.

www.hbcuconnect.com
Historically black colleges and universities

www.hacu.net
Hispanic colleges and universities

www.hillel.org
Jewish student life

www.Knowhow2go.org
This is the link from the federal government's financial aid site. Besides the college search, this site has links to all kinds of information about college planning.

http://nces.ed.gov/collegenavigator/
National Center for Educational Statistics College Navigator

The college search engines will allow your kid to search for schools through different filters. Examples are location, student population, majors, and cost. Though there are many search engines out there that will help your kid learn about colleges and universities, I've listed what I know are reliable ones. Be careful of recruitment scams. There are people eagerly waiting to exploit parents and students for personal profit. They claim to help kids find the best schools, but are out to grab your money. Searching for colleges isn't hard, but does take time.

Your kid can also find printed material within the professional school counselor's office or in his college and career center.

College Entrance Exams

You may not know this, but when your kid takes the ACT or SAT (and their earlier assessments PLAN and PSAT), the tests have a service designed to help colleges find him. With ACT, the service is Educational Opportunity Service, abbreviated as EOS. Your kid must "opt in" to this service if he wants to be in the searchable pool. I heard stories of counselors instructing students not to be part of the service, but I believe it's to your kid's advantage to allow college access to general information about his abilities and career interests.

Colleges can search out students by geographic area, race/ethnicity, grade point average, class rank, and other categories. Every college wants to find the best fit for their school just as you want to find the best college fit for your kid. You should know that colleges look for students who tested in their junior year, or even earlier, with PLAN and PSAT test data. I suggest that your kid allows the colleges an opportunity to find him.

Professional School Counselor's Office

Have your kid stop by his professional school counselor's office and introduce himself if he hasn't already, and earlier in his high school career is better than later. Counselors have books about colleges and have helped many students make a successful transition from high school to college. Often, counselors visit colleges and universities during their summer break so they can find out what different schools have to offer.

Every year I talk with hundreds of professional school counselors at conferences, schools, and workshops that focus on college readiness issues. Workshops typically happen at college campuses because the college admission professionals have developed ongoing relationships with professional school counselors. The college people want the high school people to see new buildings and tell them about new programs at the college. Professional school counselors and college admission professionals work together to make college a reality for students. It's not a job, but a passion.

Here's where I speak in support of professional school counselors. I absolutely adore them, and nearly every single one of them I've met in my career is dedicated to helping students be successful academically and emotionally. School counselors typically have over 250 students they advise, although I've heard of up to 1,000 students for every counselor. Wow! They provide classroom programming on college issues and are ready to advise and assist students. The students who step into the counselor's offices are the most likely to receive individual attention. That's why I recommend your kid establishing contact with his counselor.

Career Centers on High School Campuses
A current trend in providing students with college and career information at high school campuses is the development of career centers on either individual campuses or at a center within the school district. One primary goal of the career centers is to help students make the connection between education and careers. In meeting this goal, they provide information to students about colleges and universities. Often, career centers offer students computer access to search for schools. Staff assists students with searches, applications, financial aid, and scholarships. I'll talk about scholarships and financial aid later.

College Recruitment Counselors

Many colleges have large recruitment offices staffed with recent graduates from their school. Who best to talk about a college than a recent graduate, right? They want to find the right match for their college just as you want to find the best college for your kid. These folks can speak from a personal perspective about what college life is like and they know how the admissions process works. They work a specific territory so that they also develop relationships with the local school counselors.

I have to add a personal note. These recent graduates are too cool. They throw their hearts in their work and love the school they represent. These folks travel the highways like you cannot believe and don't make much money in the process. It's usually their first job after graduation. I adore their enthusiasm and dedication. If you meet one, please understand that they are the best of the best. They love their college, and they love people.

The college counselors meet with prospective students at high schools. They answer questions and are there to help your kid through the process of college admissions. These recruitment counselors even cross state lines to work with students from different areas. In a large state like Texas, a recruitment counselor for the University of Texas at Austin may actually live in the Dallas area and work with schools in that area. Texas Tech has an office in San Antonio.

Your kid can establish a working relationship with a college admission counselor working at the colleges on his list. This should happen either by him visiting with that recruitment officer when he/she is on your kid's high school campus or by calling the college and finding out who his representative is.

College Fairs/College Nights
College fairs and college nights are specific events at high schools. In urban areas, there may be citywide college nights. College recruitment counselors from different postsecondary institutions show up at a high school gym or cafeteria (a convention hall in large cities) for several hours so that students and parents can meet and talk with a college representative. You will often find school representatives from an entirely different region of the country represented at college fairs. College recruitment counselors may recruit heavily in your region or they may have alumnus answering questions.

The college fairs I'm most familiar with are located in Texas. Each year, the Texas Association for College Admission Counseling (www.tacac.org) organizes a series of college fairs (they have to print a book with all the cities and dates). The college recruitment counselors travel from one city to the next; they attend fairs and answer questions about their colleges. They host big events during the evening and smaller ones at specific schools during the days. These fairs start in September and end before the Christmas holiday. Think of it as the college admission traveling show. They start back up again during the spring and target high school juniors.

I've attended enough college fairs to tell you they are great family events if you have more than one child. That said; don't go expecting one-on-one attention from recruiters from popular schools. They're swamped. I've seen tables surrounded by students and parents; sixty or seventy people waiting to ask a question and pick up information or grab some of the goodies the colleges give away. It is a great place to pick up information and find a recruitment officer to contact later.

Check out the following national Web site to find out about college nights and fairs. Call your kid's professional school counselor and see what is scheduled in your area.

www.nacacnet.org
National Association for College Admission Counseling
> This is a great resource for all kinds of good information about the college admission process. They even have a college application fee waiver for students who qualify.

http://www.nacacnet.org/STUDENTINFO/FEEWAIVER/Pages/default.aspx
NACAC fee waiver form

Have your kid develop a spreadsheet or some system of keeping track of all the schools of interest. Include columns for location, cost, admission criteria, application requirements, admission test requirements, and application and financial aid deadlines. I would even suggest having him develop a second system (a college diary—either written or on a computer) where he can list his thoughts and impressions that don't easily translate to a spreadsheet format.

I know I wrote that once before. I wrote it again because I think it is important for you and your kid to stay organized throughout the high school to college transition.

Finished Shopping and Sampling Hors D'oeuvres?
It's Time to Select the Main Course: Narrowing the College Choice

The truth is your kid will invest years and thousands of dollars at college. If it's not the right fit, those few years may begin to feel like a lifetime and end without graduation. I don't want that. I jokingly tell people the worst way to choose a school is, "I want to go to (insert college name) because my (boyfriend, girlfriend, best friend) goes there."

Pleeeease! If it's true love, it will last. If not, college remains a great place for new adventures and friendships.

There Are Many Ways to Pick a School So Let's Start with a Few Questions

Will your kid do better in a class with 200 other people, or 25?
HINT: Some students thrive in lecture halls while others don't.

I once sat in a class with 700 other students and the first words the professor said were, "Don't talk to me. Talk to the teaching assistant first." He was a famous scientist and concentrated on research. He had to teach a class or two, but he didn't want to interact with anyone other than whom he chose. Many students hoped to become scientists and wanted to hear a famous scientist share theories and research. I was lost.

Does your kid know exactly what he wants to do with the rest of his life?
This is a huge question. Some kids do, while others don't have a clue. Many kids only think they know what they want to do and will change majors several times. Some people, like my father, knew from an early age what he wanted from life. He worked on an oilrig in Oklahoma as a teenager and wanted to be the boss on one. He spent over forty years as a petroleum engineer—the boss of the boss of the person who ran the rigs.

If your kid knows or has an idea of how he wants to spend his life, he should choose a school that offers a pathway to that career. He may even want to research what schools have the best programs for the area he wants to study.

Does your kid need to be close to home or is he mature enough to attend school far away?
This isn't the time to weep over thoughts of him leaving. What I'm asking is what the level of your kid's maturity is? Can your kid get up in the morning without you nagging him? Can he put his clothes on and arrive where he needs to be on time? There's no person at college forcing him to go to class or telling him to do his homework.

Would your kid do better in a small town, suburban area, or busy city?
I remember staying in London during a summer abroad program. I saw plays, visited museums, died my hair purple, and soaked up pub culture. After two weeks, this small town girl was ready to head for the country where I didn't hear the sound of sirens, cars, and airplanes. That same quiet that I long for drives other people crazy.

What kind of activities and support does the school offer?
If your kid has played sports, volunteered for community service projects, been active in school government, or mentored others, does the school offer the extracurricular activities that would interest him?

Cookbook for Getting Your Kid to College

What kinds of academic support does the school offer?

It's best to know the types of additional help the school offers. Most schools have some sort of learning center. Some teachers will even refer students for help if they think the student is in trouble of not passing. Have your kid check out how much emphasis is put into making sure he passes his classes. If your kid has special needs (ADHD, for example), college is very different from high school. Your kid now has to take responsibility for finding the services he needs.

How much does the school cost?

Yes, you have a right to ask the question. You and your kid are making a major financial investment. You might faint from sticker shock when you start adding up the tuition, fees, books, living expenses, and incidentals. College costs continue to rise. I'm going to explain more about costs and financial aid later, but it's always good to compare the cost of one school to another. Don't rule out a school because you think you'll have to sell Great Aunt Margaret's silver service to pay for it. Over 70% of students attending postsecondary education receive some form of financial aid.

Final Thoughts

Finally, ask your kid what gut feeling he has or what he thinks about each school that's a favorite. I don't mean grill him, but help him think through the process of determining the good, bad, and ugly of each school. Don't accept "I don't know" as an answer. To quote my favorite rock 'n' roll star, Tom Petty, "This is an adult conversation."

While Web sites allow great access to virtual tours, they are no substitute for a campus visit. When your kid gets serious about a couple of different schools, schedule a trip to each if you can. I've heard of kids sure about a particular school until arriving and seeing it in person. After touring the campus, they knew within the first hour that it wasn't a match. I'm not advocating weekend jet trips across the country. While personal trips do provide great information, these activities are usually reserved for parents and students with time to college shop. Some high schools actually take students to tour colleges and many host weekend visits for potential students and their parents. They have scheduled programs that address what you and your kid need to know. Often, your kid will even spend the night in a dorm room. Visit your son's professional school counselor's office to see if the school sponsors such trips.

This is where the college search spreadsheet and notes pay off. Having all information discussed above at his fingertips, means your kid doesn't have to keep going back to the Internet to find out information.

Kitchen Time: Preparing the Kitchen Makes Cooking the Main Course Easier
Your Kid and College Entrance Exams

First, what's the reasoning behind a college entrance exam? Their goal is to predict the ability of any student to do well during his first year of college. This is a process of evaluating students under standard conditions. Colleges typically use the test results in combination with high school grade point average (GPA) and class rank to determine if a student is accepted. Some schools also look at student essays, letters of recommendation, personal interviews, and if anyone in your family has attended the college (legacy).

Basically what happens in the testing situation is that students gather together to take a test in a set amount of time. These are the standard conditions. The tests are scored and reflect back to the student, parent, and college how the student performed against the group.

Why do standardized tests such as the ACT or SAT exist? A big reason is that if colleges looked only at grade point average (GPA) and class rank, they would be operating under the assumption that a 4.0 grade point average from one high school equaled the same as a 4.0 grade point average from a high school across all towns, states, or the country.

You and I both know that one high school can be much more academically challenging than the next, just as kids know that taking Ms. Jone's Algebra I class is much more difficult than taking Mr. Smith's Algebra I class. Remember when you were a kid and knew how one teacher was harder than another was? It's the same sort of idea. College entrance exams give colleges the ability to compare students under the same conditions.

That said there is controversy surrounding standardized tests such as the ACT and SAT. A small number of schools adhere to a practice known as "test optional". These schools don't require a standardized test score and admit students using the things I already listed (GPA, class rank, essays, and others). Each college's

Website will define what needs to be sent for consideration of admission.

When is the best time to take a college entrance exam? At the end of the student's junior year. The April through June test dates are for junior testing. When a kid takes an entrance exam for the first time during his senior year, he doesn't have much time to work on improving his score before college application deadlines begin approaching. That's a big issue if he's not happy with his score. Several states pay for an entrance exam for high school juniors. They do this to encourage college readiness. Remember, I already told you colleges don't target seniors when they recruit using standardized test information.

ACT or SAT?
Let's examine both. Couldn't resist the pun!

The ACT is a curriculum-based achievement test in English, math, reading, and science, and includes an optional writing test. Curriculum-based means that your kid will be tested on the academic skills that he should be learning in his high school classes. The harder and more advanced the courses are that he takes, as well as his meeting the requirements of the class (doing homework and studying for tests), the better he's going to do on The ACT Assessment. The English, math, reading, and science tests are each scored on a 1 to 36 range. To figure out the composite score, add the fours tests together, divide by four, and round to the nearest number.

Remember that the writing test is optional. Have your kid check the colleges he plans to apply to so he can determine if they require the writing test. When in doubt, take the writing test. If he needs it and doesn't have it, he will have to take the entire test again.

According to the SAT Web site, "The SAT tests the reading, writing, and math skills that you learn in school and that are critical for success in college and beyond."

The SAT has three sections, and each is scored on a scale of 400 to 800. The top score on the SAT used to be 1600. With the addition of the third section on writing, the top score is now 2400. When you were in high school, you might remember that the top score was 1600 but that is no longer true. The top score on each assessment is still 800. A total score is obtained by adding the three test scores together.

Those are the basics.

Next, I have a resource that shows how the tests stack up against each other. This comparison comes from Learn More Indiana. I wanted to find a Web site that wasn't from either a testing organization or a for-profit company and this is one of the best. This site also has a link titled ACT/SAT Reference Sheet. Click on it to find how an ACT score translates to an SAT score:

```
http://www.learnmoreindiana.org/college
/applying/AdmissionsRequirements/Pages
/ACT_SAT.aspx
```

Understand that the writing section of the ACT is optional. Why? Most schools don't require a standardized writing test. The reason is many colleges, if they require a writing sample at all, ask for it in the form of an application essay or they have developed a writing tool through their own English departments.

My advice is if your kid knows what college he wants to attend and no writing test is required, don't take it. If he doesn't know where he wants to go, then your kid should take the writing test. I know you just read about this. When you see something three times, it's because I think it's important. I want your kid to make the right choice regarding ACT's essay.

Area	ACT	SAT
Mathematics	60-question, 60-minute test. Measures mathematical skills most students have learned in courses taken by the end of 11th grade. Questions focus on algebra, geometry, and trigonometry. Questions are multiple-choice and require knowledge of basic formulas and computational skills. *Both the ACT and SAT allow students to use a four-function, scientific, or graphing calculator during the math test, but models with certain features are prohibited.*	70 minutes taken in two 25-minute sections and one 20-minute section Tests math topics such as: numbers and operations, algebra and functions, geometry, statistics, probability, and data analysis. Questions are multiple-choice and student-produced responses. Student-produced responses have no answer choices provided. Instead, the answers are filled in on a special grid. Ten questions will be of this type.
Reading	40-question, 35-minute test. Questions are multiple-choice. Measures reading comprehension through several texts and questions that show an understanding of what is directly stated and what is implied.	70 minutes taken in two 25-minute sections and one 20-minute section. The critical reading section includes short reading passages along with the existing long reading passages. Analogies have been eliminated, but sentence-completion questions and passage-based reading questions remain.

Area	ACT	SAT
English	75-question, 45-minute test. Questions are multiple-choice. Measures standard written English (punctuation, grammar usage, and sentence structure) and rhetorical skills (strategy, organization, and style).	The SAT does not have a separate English section, but the multiple-choice questions in the writing section measure ability to improve sentences and paragraphs as well as find errors (diction, grammar, sentence construction, subject-verb agreement, word usage, and wordiness).
Science	40-question, 35-minute test. Questions are multiple-choice. Measures skills in the natural sciences: interpretation, analysis, evaluation, reasoning, and problem-solving. Assumes students have completed a course in biology as well as a course in an earth science and/or physical science.	The SAT does not test Science.
Writing	30-minute essay test that measures writing skills emphasized in high school English classes and in entry-level college composition courses. The essay involves responding to a question about a particular issue described in the writing prompt.	Multiple-choice questions (35 minutes) and student-written essay (25 minutes). The short essay measures ability to: clearly organize, express, develop, and support ideas, and use appropriate word choices and sentence structures.

Which Test Should Your Kid Take?

The fact is almost every college in the country will accept both. There are a few exceptions. More schools prefer the ACT to the SAT. Many highly competitive colleges will take ACT scores instead of the SAT combined with SAT II subject tests.

Find out the policies of the schools in which your kid is most interested. I'll cover SAT IIs later.

Here's the deal. Colleges and universities use a conversion chart to convert SAT scores to ACT scores or ACT scores to SAT scores. Here's a link to the chart:

http://www.act.org/aap/concordance/

You don't need to become an expert in testing, but I thought you might find the link helpful.

Most schools take the highest score of either the ACT or SAT and use that score for admission purposes. I hear professional school counselors tell students to take one or both. If happy with a score, no further testing is needed. If your kid is not happy with his score, pick one and work on making the result better.

This brings me to a dreaded topic that I'm only going to touch on briefly—superscoring. Some schools use this practice. They take the highest score from each section of either the ACT or SAT (pulling scores from across multiple test administrations) and use it to form their own composite. Neither ACT nor College Board advocates for this practice, but colleges do it. One testing tactic for schools that engage in superscoring is to have your kid send two sets of test scores (either ACT or SAT or both) so the schools have a choice of which scores to use.

Let me illustrate this practice. Your kid sends two ACT scores to XYZ University. He scores a 23 on the English test the first time and a 24 when he took it a second time. The second time he took the test, his math score dropped two points. With superscoring, XYZ University would use his highest English and highest math score even though they came from different test dates.

Here's my problem with superscoring. Kids have to take tests multiple times. Both ACT and SAT provide fee waivers to families that can't afford to pay (based on income—not because someone is cash-strapped one particular month). The kid who takes a test four or five times has the opportunity to do better via superscoring than the kid who can't afford to test beyond the use of fee waivers.

You will find that some states are now testing entire grade levels (currently grade 11) with either the ACT, SAT, or giving the student a choice. Illinois started the practice, followed by Colorado. Lucky you, if you live in one of the states helping students prepare for college.

Here's my best answer. Have your kid choose either the ACT or SAT or have him take both. If he's happy with his score, he's done. If not, try again—either with the same test or with the other one.

Yes, I know it's time and money. If your kid qualifies for free or reduced lunch (because of income and not because the whole school is on free lunch), then your kid qualifies for both an ACT and a SAT fee waiver. He can take each test twice without paying for them. Your kid's professional school counselor will have fee waivers and requirements for qualifying.

Passing or Failing the ACT or SAT

I can't believe I wrote that heading! I want to drive home this point with a story. Years ago, I watched a Ken Burns documentary, Country Boys, detailing the hardships two boys from Appalachia faced on their path to adulthood.

I'm sitting in front of the television bawling my eyes out, just sobbing over the poverty and alcoholism in the area. Both boys were starting their college planning path (way late if you ask me). One of the boys looked at the camera and said, "I failed my ACT." My crying stopped immediately. I jumped from my chair, screaming at the set, "Nooooooo!" I scared my husband who had been laughing at my crying.

The next day, I searched the internet about Ken Burns. I called his production team to find out what school the boys attended. I packed up college readiness information materials to send to the boys' school.

The point is there is no passing or failing of the ACT or SAT. Instead, the question to ask is if your kid's score is competitive enough to allow entrance to the school of his dreams. Most schools combine test scores with class rank and grade point average to make decisions about admission; there is no 'passing' or 'failing.'

SAT II or the ACT

Many of the most competitive schools (the hard ones to be accepted into) require SAT IIs. These are additional tests on specific subjects. Schools may or may not suggest which subject tests to take. The requirement of SAT IIs should be listed on the spreadsheet your kid started during the college search.

Since the ACT is a curriculum-based achievement test and tests what students have covered in their high school courses, many of the same schools that require SAT IIs do not require additional tests if the student has an ACT score on file. Again, check with the colleges to find out their policy.

Time to register?

ACT: http://www.actstudent.org/

SAT: http://student.collegeboard.org

Preparing for the ACT or SAT

Did you know that both ACT and College Board (they administer the SAT) are non-for-profit organizations? Yes, they are. They make money, but it goes back into research and solutions related to helping students become college and career ready. All the test prep companies combined together translate into a billion dollar industry.

To prep or not to prep is the question. If you have unlimited resources, go for it. Otherwise, choose preparation programs carefully. Both ACT and College Board have free and low-cost resources on their Web sites to help students prepare.

ACT: http://www.actstudent.org/

SAT: http://student.collegeboard.org

Check out the resources your kid's school has to help him prepare for college entrance exams. Most schools offer something. I've witnessed many outstanding school programs as I've visited high schools. Some schools have even purchased expensive prep programs for all their students.

Five Final Points on College Entrance Exams

I could write a book on test prep. If you've looked at the test preparation section at any bookstore or searched the Internet, you will determine I couldn't add anything new.

1. I would highly suggest retesting if your student is one or two points away from a scholarship opportunity at the school of his choice. Example: Your kid has a 27 composite on the ACT, and XYZ University offers a $4,000 merit scholarship for students who score a 28.
2. If your kid needs extended time or any kind of testing accommodations, contact your professional school counselor to start the paperwork. Don't wait until the day before the test's registration deadline. You might have the accommodation approved in time, but if there are questions or additional paperwork is requested, time could run short. It's the school professional's job to help students complete the paperwork for accommodations, but it is up to ACT and the College Board to determine if a student qualifies. The goal of accommodations is to provide fair testing to all students.
3. There are no shortcuts to preparing for college entrance exams. Be aware of those test prep businesses or books promising to increase your kid's scores by huge gains. The best way to prepare is for your kid to take the hardest classes he can handle.
4. When your kid is studying test questions for either test, realize the goal is to become

familiar with the types of questions found on the test (yes, that kind of practice helps), but it's no substitute for being able to figure out the answer to a math problem.
5. Good practice for the ACT is to take PLAN at grade 10. Good practice for the SAT is to take the PSAT at grade 11.

Been reading about people being paid to take the SAT for someone else? Rest assured that both companies are taking precautions so this doesn't happen again. Test admission tickets will now have a student photo on them.

Tell your kid I wish him the best on whichever exam he takes.

Picking Out a Choice Cut of Meat
Applying to College

Here's where you lean on your kid to start working hard. By this time, he should have searched colleges, far and near, and determined if his chances of acceptance are likely or not. He may have visited those colleges on his short list. He should have created a spreadsheet or some other system to keep track of the colleges he's most interested in, as well as their application deadlines. This is not the time to rely on memory.

Your kid needs to divide his college list into three groups. He may need help with this process. Some kids may engage in wishful thinking or believe that every college would be happy to have him. The first category is those colleges that will be a stretch for him to be accepted at. The second category is of schools where he has a reasonable good chance of acceptance. The last group is of schools he knows will accept him—these are his backup or safety net colleges. This is where the spreadsheet and notes he developed during his college search pay off. He can look back at the information without having to return time after time to the schools' Web sites. Even if your kid knows exactly which school he wants to attend, I suggest a backup college. It's smart because not everything works out as one hopes and plans.

How Long Does the Meat Need to Marinade?
Admission Acceptance Plans

Regular Application Decision
Your kid is in the mix with all the other kids who applied by the regular application deadline. If accepted, your kid is not obligated to attend the college. Your kid might have applied to ten schools and been accepted to all of them. If so, it's his time to choose.

Rolling Admission
Your kid applies and the school accepts or rejects him as the application is received. Your kid isn't being compared to the entire application pool. When the number of slots allocated

for the freshman class is filled, the school stops accepting students.

Early Decision
Your kid knows the school he wants to attend, and he applies by their early deadline. If accepted, process over. Your kid may not apply to more than one school for early admission. By applying for Early Decision, your kid has committed to attending that college if he is accepted. Did you read that? He can only apply to one school under the early decision program and acceptance is binding. The only way he won't be bound to the decision is if they college doesn't offer enough financial aid for him to attend. Let me assure that the world of college admission professionals is really a small one. I have heard of kids who have tried to scam the early admission application by applying to more than one school. Upon being caught, the student was denied admission to both schools.

Under Early Decision, students have earlier application deadlines (usually in November of the senior year). Students also find out if they are accepted earlier than other students (as early as December).

Early Action
This one is similar to Early Decision but is not binding. Also your kid can apply to more than one school under Early Action.

Sound confusing? It is! These different plans bring controversy to the college admission process. Some schools are doing away with all their admission categories, but there are still many colleges that still use them.

You also need to know what the term "wait list" means. You can likely guess! I consider it to be college admission limbo. The college has neither accepted nor rejected a student. They are likely waiting to see how many students they have offered admission accept and the offer. Remember that some kids are applying to six or more schools, but they can only enroll in one.

Combining All the Ingredients
Pulling the Meal Together
College Applications

Find college applications online in the admission section of each college or university. Once your kid has completed one, have him print it out and save it. He's going to need the same information repeatedly.

The good news is that many colleges subscribe to what is known as the Common Application. This is one-stop shopping and one application works for many different schools, especially private schools. At the Common Application Web site, the different colleges will also list the supplemental information they require. Have your kid check to see if any of his college choices use the common application. Currently, over 450 colleges use the same application. The common application also has six college essay prompts from which students may choose.

Common Application
https://www.commonapp.org/CommonApp/default.aspx
EDU, Inc.

Common Black College Application
http://www.eduinconline.com/
   This site allows students to apply to over thirty historically black colleges and universities (HBCU) with one application and for one application fee.

Other Common Applications
Several states and college systems have their own common applications. For example, Texas has one common application for all public schools in the state. The State University of New York system has an application that works for all the universities in their system. The best way to find out if the schools on your kid's list participate in some form of common application is to check their admission Web site. You can also Google the state's department of higher education. Search "state name department of higher education."

```
https://www.applytexas.org/adappc/en
/c _ start.WBX
```
Apply Texas

College Essays
You or your kid can find a large selection of books that help with writing college entrance essays online and at your local bookstore. I'd like to add two tips about application essays. If your kid's school choices require them, your kid needs to write something interesting. Picture a roomful of admission professionals sitting around a table, marathon-reading essay after essay. Wouldn't you want to read something different from the previous ten essays you had just finished reading, if you were one of those admissions people? Original attracts attention. My second piece of advice is to start writing early. Don't let your kid wait until the weekend before it's due. Writing is rewriting. Follow the rewriting with revisions and polish. As an example, I've reworked the writing in this guide more times than I can count. I've had other people look it over to find what I've left out, and I've paid someone to proofread it.

Check out sample essays by doing a Google search on "college application essays." There are multitudes of free sample essays. College Board has samples on their student Web site. I looked at Amazon.com and found dozens of books on the subject, but I'm not making any recommendations. Once again, a trip to the professional school counselor's office or career center might unearth a wealth of additional free resources.

Be careful, college admission essays are another way unscrupulous people try to part you from your money by offering to sell you an essay. There are also people who, for a fee, will provide consultation editing (I'm not talking about them). Tell your kid to ask his English teacher if she will help him with the essay. Maybe your cousin is married to an English teacher. Ask that person for assistance. Most people really want to help when kids begin their college journeys.

I'm a writer. I've written two novels (see KiowaHillPublishing.com). I consider myself somewhat knowledgeable on writing. Let me tell you, writing is rewriting is rewriting is rewriting. The essays that rise to the surface are polished and shaped by multiple drafts. Have I said that before?

College Application Fees
Times have changed and many schools charge a fee to apply to their institution.

This is a way to raise money for school budgets that have been slashed. It also helps pay for time devoted to essay reading and processing applications. Some schools are receiving over a hundred applications for every student accepted. That translates into thousands of hours devoted to the admission process. Some schools will waive application fees if the students help them streamline the admission process by applying online.

If your kid qualifies for an ACT or SAT fee waiver, he qualifies for a college application fee waiver unless something prohibits schools from accepting fee waivers. For an ACT or SAT college application fee waiver, ask your professional school counselor. In addition, the National Association for College Admission Counseling (NACAC) has a fee waiver that works for both tests.

http://www.nacacnet.org/studentinfo
/feewaiver/Pages/default.aspx
NACAC fee waiver Web site

College application fees can add up to hundreds of dollars if your kid is applying to several schools. If your budget can handle it, go for it. If not, this may be the time to further narrow the application field.

High School Grades

Colleges and universities don't take a student's word about his high school grades. They want official transcripts. Your kid will need to request his grades through his high school registrar or whoever else deals with high school transcripts. Your kid typically cannot put in his request for a transcript the day before the application deadline and expect the school to copy and mail it that day. Some high schools will post how many days they need to process a transcript request.

Most colleges will want to see your kid's grades for the end of his first senior semester as well as his final grades upon graduation. Early admission decisions may be based on grades through his junior year. I have recently started hearing of colleges basing acceptance on first semester senior grades, but with a disclaimer that they have a right to revoke acceptance based upon the senior's second semester grades. Translated, they don't want kids blowing off their last semester of high school because they've made it into the college of their choice. They want students who are dedicated and working hard all the way through their senior year.

Letters of Recommendation

Not every college requires letters of recommendation. This is where that spreadsheet of each college's requirements will come in handy. If a letter or letters are needed, the first step is to figure out whom to ask. Of course, it is best if it's a teacher who knows your kid and can write nice words about him.

Have your kid make it easy for anyone who is writing a letter of recommendation. A summary sheet that your kid has written about his high school accomplishments and goals can help.

Give the letter-writer time to write, and I don't mean a week before the deadline. Give the writer at least a month (the more time the better for the letter writer). Have your kid develop a packet that gives him an edge over other students. This includes the letter deadline, summary of his student accomplishments, a stamped and addressed envelope for the writer to use, and any forms the college may require with the recommendation.

If someone says he/she can't write the letter, find someone else who is willing to write it. The person may be swamped with writing other letters or maybe doesn't like your kid as much as your kid thought he did. I'm kidding about the person not liking your kid. I have talked with teachers who take college recommendation letter writing very seriously. They may feel they have already committed to the maximum number of letters they can write or maybe they don't know your kid well enough to write a letter that will show his skills in the best possible light.

Wouldn't it be nice if after someone wrote a personalized letter of recommendation for your kid that he had the courtesy to send a hand-written thank you note to the person who wrote it?

Details, Details, Details

Every college is unique and can ask for different requirements from potential students.

I started back to school for a second master's degree. This one was a master of fine arts in creative writing. Would you believe I had to submit thirty pages of sample fiction with my application? I can't imagine an art school not wanting to see sample artwork or a music school not wanting a sample of voice or instrument. These are portfolios of student work.

Remember, it is your kid's responsibility to send in all the materials required by the posted deadlines. Your kid may get a pass if a teacher's letter of recommendation was late. He will likely not be considered if he's the one not submitting his application materials on time. Meeting deadlines speaks to your kid's ability to follow through. If your kid can't meet the application deadline, do you think the school believes he will turn in his assignments on time? He's becoming an adult and he's playing in the adult world.

One final tip that may help. I suggest students develop a resume of their high school and community activities and accomplishments. If he does this every year he's in high school, he won't forget something important on his college application. This really helps in remembering what has happened during his entire high school career.

The Kitchen Heat
All those college applications are in the mail, right? Good job! Now it's time to wait, wait, and

wait even more. Between the college entrance exams and application acceptance letters, many of today's kids are living in a world of college acceptance anxiety. It's tough! You're probably feeling the anxiety with him since you've been helping your kid with the process. I wish there was something I could say that would ease the process for both of you, but I don't think there is. The best I can offer is that you both try and focus on other issues. The letters from colleges will start arriving soon enough. I hope it is good news for you both.

Paying for the Meal
Finding Money for Your Kid's College

I know you meant to put money away each month for your kid's college fund, and maybe you did. If so, congratulations! For some people, life's emergencies required skimming money off the college fund to put food on the table. Maybe you did manage to squirrel away money from each paycheck, but who could have expected the tuition and fees explosion over the past decades?

College remains one of the biggest monetary investments you'll make in your kid. It's the last step to launching him into the world of adulthood. That is, unless you bought him a Bentley or other high-end graduation present. If your kid drives a car costing over $50,000, skip this section. For the rest of you, read on.

I want to share a story of a dear friend. She did the whole thing of saving for her son's college the right way. She started putting money into his college fund when she was pregnant. She paid into that account before she put money towards any other bills or expenses. She delivered the college expectation message as he grew up (very important to set those expectations). She made him take the hard classes in high school. Way to go! She stayed involved in everything he did.

This isn't the story of a trained stockbroker. This woman worked as an oil and gas secretary and survived periodic episodes of unemployment. Her own education involved a year of college, but she left school because with three jobs, she found herself falling asleep in class. As her son stepped across his high school graduation stage, she had saved about $20,000 to pay for college. Impressive! I think so. That wound up paying for about one year at a private university and that was years ago. Today, kids can graduate with a bachelor's degree and owe tens of thousands of dollars in student loans.

Here's the deal! Unless you can pay for every penny of your kid's education, you and your kid will need to complete the Free Application for Federal Student Aid (FAFSA). You both can fill it out online and the Web site is:

```
http://www.fafsa.ed.gov
```

I made the URL huge so you can find it when you're flipping through this text. From this primary government Web site, you can link to many of the Web sites I will explain regarding the FAFSA.

Completing the FAFSA:
Free Application for Federal Student Aid

You and your kid will need to start applying for financial as quickly as possible, but not before January 1 of your kid's senior year. Save your last pay stubs (his too if he has a job) because you can estimate income on the FAFSA and then go back and make corrections later if needed. I hope you can read bluntness here. Start early! Don't put it off! Make it your New Year's resolution! The buck starts here! Make like Nike's slogan and DO IT!

Do you get it? You *need* to complete your tax forms as early as possible. I didn't say you have to file your tax forms, but you *must* complete the FAFSA. Why? Colleges provide the best financial aid packages to those students who meet their deadlines and financial aid deadlines come early. Financial aid deadlines can be different dates than the application deadline.

Your kid's financial need is determined by your ability to pay for his education. That's it, the bottom line, and the end of the story!

It doesn't matter if you don't think you should pay for his education because the government says that it is a parent responsibility. They control the money. If you want any chance of your kid receiving governmental aid, you both must fill out the FAFSA.

Remember all the rush and pressure regarding your kid's college application deadlines? This isn't as bad, but almost. Just as colleges have deadlines for admission, they have priority deadlines for financial aid.

Colleges have limited dollars to award to students in the form of grants and scholarships, and the students who meet their deadline are in the mix for the best awards. Those other kids, the ones who missed the financial aid deadlines, receive monies left over after the first round of awards is given. Of course, most government money is based on your ability to pay.

Let me come at if from a different angle. Colleges receive dollar allocations from the federal government that they award to students in grants, loans, and work-study. Schools run out of money. The kid who applies late could be eligible for a grant (free money) based on his FAFSA, but the school doesn't have any more of that particular grant money to offer. That's the student who ends up with more loans.

Different states also have deadlines for applying for financial aid, but these are much later than the college deadlines. At the FAFSA Web site, you can check the state deadlines:

http://www.fafsa.ed.gov/deadlines.htm.

Creating a PIN
Before completing the FAFSA, you and your kid must go to the Web site and create an account:

http://www.pin.ed.gov/PINWebApp/pinindex.jsp

Once that's done, you may have to wait a day or two for the account to be set up.

From the PIN application site:

> Your PIN can be used each year to apply electronically [sic] for federal student aid and to access your Federal Student Aid records online. If you receive a PIN, you agree not to share it with anyone. Your PIN serves as your electronic signature and provides access to your personal records, so you should never give your PIN to anyone, including commercial services that offer to help you complete your FAFSA. Be sure to keep your PIN in a safe place.

After receiving a PIN, gather all your financial documents together. Start filling out the FAFSA. You don't have to complete it all at once. You can save your data and come back later to finish. It's not painful, but is time consuming. Do it ASAP!

Once you're done, all the information you put in is combined to determine your Expected Family Contribution (EFC). This information is sent to you online in the form of a Student Aid Report (SAR). The calculation to determine how much aid your kid is eligible to receive is complex. It includes such things as how close the oldest parent is to retirement, house mortgage payments, business loss or gain, your kid's income from work, and number of people in school (including parents). It doesn't include your credit card debt or car payments. You buying that dream car or turning your kid's room into a den might have to wait a little longer.

Now you have an EFC (expected family contribution). The EFC doesn't change (usually). What does change is the cost of each school your kid considers. For ease of math, let's say your EFC is $2,500. That means this year you are expected to contribute $2,500 toward your kid's education during his upcoming academic year. Now let's examine the cost of three different schools over an academic year.

	Community College	State College	Private University
Tuition, fees, books, room, board, transportation, & incidentals	$5,000	$15,000	$30,000
EFC (It doesn't change)	$2,500	$2,500	$2.500
Unmet need	$2,500	$12,500	$27,500

Do you see how this works? The Cost Of Attendance (COA) of each school is the difference in the equation listed above that effects the unmet need, not the family contribution. The community college is the least expensive while the private university costs the most. COA minus EFC determines unmet financial need.

Remember you read that colleges have financial aid priority deadlines? Check with your kid's favorite school choices (or all of his hopefuls) and get the FAFSA to them before their deadlines. Your kid may also need to fill out the college's own financial aid paperwork or application, and he must finish it by any deadlines posted. Some colleges and universities (mostly private) require filling out College Board's CCS Financial Aid Profile. This profile is completed online and asks for additional information to what is on the FAFSA. There is a fee charged to complete the profile as well as a charge to send it to each college requiring it.

https://profileonline.collegeboard.com
/prf/index.jsp

Just so you and your kid can be clear on this fact: school financial aid applications are totally different from applications for admission. Each application can have its own deadline.

Remember that spreadsheet or information management system I suggested your kid develop? Now you can see why it's important. Have your kid add a line so that he can check off forms he has completed and sent to the different colleges. If you can take him out for pizza as a reward for all his hard work on the applications and financial aid, do it. You and he can use this time to discuss the different colleges still on his list. If it's a family night with younger kids along, the dinner discussion can be devoted to college issues.

Some counselors believe your kid should be completing all the admission and financial aid applications while you oversee the project. I'm of the mindset that it's a joint project. He remains the chef, but remember you are his sous-chef. Help him, support him, and encourage him. Be there for him if he's not accepted to his top college choice. Remember, he's ultimately responsible for his education, but he may need help with time management or someone to talk with about which college would be best.

Financial Aid Awards
If your kid meets all the financial aid deadlines, he will be in the school's mix for financial aid awards, assuming he's accepted to the institution. Financial aid offices work closely with admission offices.

Schools offer what is called a financial aid award package. This can be a mix of grants, work-study, and loans. A grant is money that doesn't have to be paid back. Work-study is a part-time job your kid will have at the school. I think of it as a pay as you go. A loan is money that must be repaid with interest. A loan can belong to your kid or you, depending on what type it is.

Your kid will receive an award letter from the school. You and your kid have the ability to reject and/or accept all or any part of a college's financial aid award. However, rejecting a portion doesn't mean the school will offer some other aid in its place.

As an example, let's say your kid has an uncle in the town where he will go to school. The uncle is offering your kid a weekend job that pays $20 per hour. Your kid can work one day a week with his uncle and make the same amount that he'd make working nineteen hours for the college, so he may reject the work-study portion of the award. He might work both jobs, but he needs to remember his primary job is to study and do well in class.

You both need to have a serious talk at this point. Let's say you've done all the paperwork and now your kid has been accepted to four schools, two cost around $30,000/year while the other two cost around $15,000/year. Of course, you have a community college as a backup.

Look at their financial aid award packages! Seriously, lay them out side by side and study them. How much are they offering in loans versus grants and scholarships? Simply put, how much is free money instead of money that has to be paid back? This can be the difference between you and/or your kid leaving school with a $20,000 or an $80,000 debt structure. Let's hope he graduates because loans have to be paid back regardless!

Many schools offer admission to their college in what is called "need blind" fashion. This means that when a student applies, the college makes its admission decision without knowing how much financial help the student needs. The financial aid department then works hard to come up with the best award package it can offer (assuming your kid met the financial aid deadlines).

How much do you want to dig into the topic? Look at the loans. Some accrue interest while your kid is going to school. Others provide a grace period after your kid leaves school or graduates. Don't forget to look at interest rates and any fees associated with the loan.

http://studentaid.ed.gov/PORTALSWebApp
/students/english/funding.jsp#02

Here's where I plug community colleges again. They are a cost-effective route for taking general education classes. I mean English, history, math, speech, psychology, the basic classes your kid needs before transferring to a university.

Other Helpful Facts and Web Sites

Should you want to estimate your EFC before it's time to fill out the FAFSA, there are a number of Financial Need Calculators on the internet. A good site that houses information on financial aid, scholarship searches, and financial calculators is:

http://www.finaid.org/

or go straight to:

http://fafsa4caster.ed.gov

Visit your state department of higher education's Web site. Different states have other grants and loan programs that you should know about. You can link to each state's higher education site through the FAFSA site, or directly at:

```
http://wdcrobcolp01.ed.gov/Programs/EROD
/org _ list.cfm?category _ ID=SHE
```

You can also do a Google search by "your state department of higher education." They may have an additional application to fill out, or you'll use the FAFSA.

At the FAFSA Web site, look for the explanation of the different types of loans. Some loans defer interest while others accumulate interest while your kid is in school. Some you don't pay back until after graduation while others you start paying back immediately. You and your kid need to be informed as to what each loan's obligation will be.

```
http://studentaid.ed.gov/PORTALSWebApp
/students/english/funding.jsp#02
```

Oops! Did you read that a few paragraphs ago? If you did, good for you! You're not skimming through this section. We're talking about a serious financial commitment, and I want you and your kid informed on the topic. Defaults (not paying back loan money) lead to garnishments on income tax returns and limit future access to student financial aid. Please learn what your obligations will be.

Understand that colleges are required to audit a small percentage of the FAFSA calculations and SARs (Student Aid Reports) that come to their school. You may have to take all your paperwork to your kid's college to prove to them that your income information is correct. You haven't been targeted because you or your kid did something wrong. It's random.

Remember, I wrote that it's your responsibility to pay for your kid's school. Sometimes fate deals a tragedy prior to your kid entering school. Let's say you lost your job. It happens. This means your financial picture has changed because you used the previous year's tax data for the next year's school cycle. Contact the college financial aid department and let them know what happened. They can recalculate the EFC based on this information and base aid on the new figures, but they won't know anything has changed if you don't tell them.

Complications can include a nasty divorce, your ex-spouse claiming your son for taxes, and your spouse refusing to fill out the FAFSA. My best advice is to work it out in the interest of your kid. Easier said than done? Talk to your ex-spouse's parents about what is in the best interest of their grandchild. There's no way I can tell you exactly what to do. I would suggest contacting the college and asking if they have

Cookbook for Getting Your Kid to College

any suggestions. Remember, some high schools and colleges host financial aid night to help fill out the FAFSA. Explain your specific situation and ask what they can offer as help.

Here's one last tip. When you fill out the FAFSA, money that your child has in his savings and checking account will be allocated to his education at a higher rate than the money in your savings and checking account. Why? Your kid is further away from retirement and has less financial liabilities at this time.

Helpful Financial Aid Web Sites

http://studentaid.ed.gov/students
/publications/student_guide/index.html
>   A free 52-page booklet to download in English or Spanish

http://www.college.gov/wps/portal
>   The entry portal to the government financial aid site

http://studentaid.ed.gov/PORTALSWebApp
/students/english/parents.jsp
>   Parent information on the Federal Financial Aid site

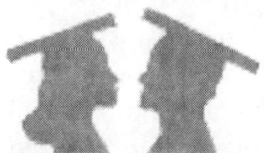

Finding Help to Pay for the Meal
Scholarship Money for Your Kid's College

There's a ton of money out there. Right? You've read the ads that tell you it's true, if you've done any scholarship searching on the Internet. You've read that thousands and thousands of dollars go unclaimed in scholarship monies each year. I've actually heard two people tell me this in one week. You and your kid have now seen the price tag of a college education.

You may have rolled away from the computer, put your hand to your heart, and cursed the emergencies that took all the extra savings you had planned to use for college expenses. Maybe now you are really staring at your Great Aunt Margaret's heirloom silver and wondering what you could get for it at those places that pay cash for gold and silver.

Guess what? You are the newest crop of ripe fruit ready for scholarship scam picking! Believe me, there are plenty of people out in cyber-land or in your own backyard waiting to pluck your dollars and sell you a scholarship search package. Step away. Step away right now. Don't give them any time to show you what they can offer with the promise that you don't have to commit until later. I really want you to picture sharks circling around a school of sardines (scammers swarming around recent high school graduates). See what the Federal Trade Commission has to say about these practices:

http://www.ftc.gov/bcp/edu/microsites/scholarship/

If a scholarship service guarantees you money or your money back, wants your bank account information, secures a scholarship that will only cost you administrative fees, or promises to do all the work for you, it's time to hold up your palm in front of your face and tell them, "Talk to the hand." If it sounds too good to be true, it's a scam. Here's one scam example that has happened repeatedly. Shark Scholarship Company (not a real company) requires a $1,000 fee to provide an individual search tailored to your kid. They guarantee results or your money back. They come back with a $200 scholarship, so they delivered on their promise and you don't get your money back. What they don't tell you is the $200 scholarship came from Baby Shark Scholarship Foundation and the parent company pocketed $800 for the ten minutes needed to transfer monies between the two companies.

Finding Money
You can do this, and furthermore, so can your kid. I'm serious. Even though I'm writing to you as the parent, this is your kid's opportunity to get invested in his college education. The entire process of searching, applying to schools, applying for financial aid and scholarships should be a joint project.

Let's debunk those advertisements you've been reading. There's truth to the claim that thousands of dollars go unclaimed. Yes, it's true. What the advertisements don't share is that the reason the monies are unclaimed is that nobody is fitting the specific requirements for a very specific set of scholarships. If your child is of a certain ethnicity, studying a certain field, hails from X state, and wants to go to Y University—this one scholarship may fit him perfectly. Those are the types of scholarships that go unclaimed and there are lots of them. The general ones are claimed every year.

Scholarships come in all shapes and sizes. They can be based on grade point average, class rank, area of study, athletics, fine arts, religious affiliation, and a whole host of other categories. They can be specific to a particular high school, town or city, state, higher education institution, or can be national.

The keys to finding scholarships is starting early, searching wide, and staying aware. When I mean early, I mean your kid's sophomore and junior year. After finding the scholarships, your kid must meet the deadlines and criteria listed.

Where to Start the Scholarship Search
Start local. First stop is your kid's high school. Many professional school counselors keep lists of what's available at the local and state level. They may subscribe to a scholarship service that will allow your student to search an extensive national database. You may need your kid to go by the office and pick up a paper list of what is available locally. That's an easy one. Many professional school counselor's have newsletters or a guidance Web site that announces upcoming scholarship deadlines. Find out what they offer.

Does your city/community have a college center? For example, San Antonio, Texas has Café College. All adults, parents, and students from around the city are welcome to come in and search the scholarship data banks. Find out if your city has a central location to help with admissions, financial aid, and scholarships. If not, or better, even still, check out your public library. See if they have or subscribe to scholarship listings.

Colleges and universities send recruitment officers out to high schools. They may come during school hours or after school (remember, I've already discussed college nights). The college recruitment activities happen during the fall semester to target seniors, and again in the spring to target juniors, but all students are welcome. The recruitment officer is a great source of information on what types of scholarships are available at their specific institution. Each college's Web site is a great source of information about the scholarships offered and the requirements.

Many states have scholarship information located with their financial aid information on their Web site. Again, do a Google search on "your state department of higher education." Find the financial aid site and see what is has to offer. A Web site that lists each higher education site is:

```
http://wdcrobcolp01.ed.gov/Programs/EROD
/org _ list.cfm?category _ ID=SHE.
```

National Scholarship Searches

Scholarships are out there and many people are looking for them. Don't be discouraged. If your kid meets the criteria, fill out the application and send in everything required.

Have your kid complete everything on the scholarship application. Don't think you can shortcut your way through the process. There are plenty of people out there ready to do what's asked. If you were on a scholarship committee and had to pick from two equal candidates, and one student sent in the required five-page essay and the other student sent only a page, whom would you pick?

Remember what I've already written about application and financial aid deadlines? The same rule holds true for scholarships.

Free Web Searches.
Here are a few scholarship Web sites I think are reputable.

https://studentaid2.ed.gov/getmoney/scholarship/v3browse.asp
> This is the federal site for finding scholarships with directions for how to use it.

http://www.collegenet.com/mach25/app
CollegeNET

http://www.scholarships.com/
Scholarships.com

http://www.finaid.org/scholarships/
> A large search engine

```
http://scholarshipamerica.org/open
_scholarships.php
```
Scholarship America
> From there, you can link to other search services.

```
https://bigfuture.collegeboard.org
/scholarship-search
```
> College Board's scholarship search

Now, it's time to roll up to the computer and start your search. Might I suggest starting a spreadsheet to keep track of scholarship names, deadlines, requirements. This is no time to rely on memory. Good luck and happy hunting!

Wait! Stop! I can hear a collective cry from those reading. Did you really think I could offer you a magic bullet? That you could punch in a Web site address and scholarships would start rolling out? I wish I had that power. The search is time consuming, but not nearly as difficult as filling out all applications required to apply for the scholarships. It's time to pull your kid back from senioritis (this may need to happen his junior year, depending on the scholarship), lounging at the beach, skiing the slopes, and cruising Main Street to shout out to his buddies. If he wants any chance at scholarship money, he's going to have to work for it.

Cookbook for Getting Your Kid to College

Think of you and your kid as a team on the path to college readiness. This is the "find the money trail" and you are both going to have to put in the hours and research for this one to have any hope of paying off.

Resource Links

http://nces.ed.gov/fastfacts/index.asp?faq=FFOption6#
National Center for Education Statistics Fast Facts
   Interesting statistics regarding secondary and postsecondary education.

http://nces.ed.gov/collegenavigator/
National Center for Education Statistics
   Features a college search. Search schools by a variety of characteristics including highest and lowest tuition costs. Great place to start an online college search.

http://www.knowhow2go.org/
>   A place to learn about planning for college readiness. This site reinforces early planning's importance to success.

http://collegecost.ed.gov/
>   Federal Web site on making the cost of postsecondary education more transparent.

http://www.educationconservancy.org/
The Education Conservancy
>   A non-profit organization dedicated to taking the frenzy out of the college admission process

www.actstudent.org
>   Great information on preparing and registering for the ACT, and research on college readiness.

http://www.nacacnet.org/studentinfo/Pages/Default.aspx
>   The NACAC site for students and parents. This is a must-see and has information available in English and Spanish

http://www.collegeboard.com
>   Register and learn more about the SAT

http://studentaid.ed.gov/PORTALSWebApp/
students/english/toolsandresources.jsp

> A government portal that will detail Web sites regarding student financial aid. I highly recommend this site for all kinds of free publications about planning for college.

There are many Web sites out there to help. I've only listed the ones I've visited and feel comfortable sending you to. As you can probably tell, I don't want be the one telling you about all the companies that will help for a fee. If that's the route you and your kid decide to take, there will be no problem for you to find your path there. May I just say, please be careful.

If you do decide to hire someone to help you and your kid with the process, check with your professional school counselors to determine if they have recommendations. Another Web site to visit for a list of private college counselors who can help is:

http://www.iecaonline.com/
Independent Educational Consultants Association

> They have names of counselors who have spent their professional years helping students. These counselors adhere to a code of ethics, keep updated about college admission practices, and have completed a list of requirements to join the organization.

Relax and Enjoy the Meal

We need several plates to serve all the courses needed for the meal of finding, applying, and paying for college. I wish this were an easy meal to prepare. I've taken over making Thanksgiving at my parents' house as they have aged. I feel as if that day, I prepare and prep, and the truth is, all I'm doing is heating stuff that has been bought already made. When the meal is ready (hopefully everything at the same time), everyone sits at the table. We probably eat 4,000 calories in twenty minutes. Think of all the courses served in this book as preparing for your kid's college feast. Luckily, it's not over in 20 minutes.

You are launching your precious child onto a major path toward adulthood. The better prepared you both are, the smoother the process will be and the more likely he will successfully make the transition. If you have more than one kid, the great news is with the next one, you will be a pro.

I wish you both the best in this process. Call this my blessing on your kid's college feast. You didn't see me writing this, but if you did, you would see that right now I have tears in my eyes. I want your kid to do well. I really do. I want every child who enters college to love the experience and use the education to launch him onto the path of his dreams.

Wouldn't it be cool if every person graduated from college into a job that fulfilled the work portion of his life? I think so. I believe everyone needs to find work and personal balance in life. I want your kid to find passion in his existence and to love what he does (and the same for you).

Please let me know if this book helped you and your kid. I'd also love to hear about your experiences on any of the topics I've covered. Remember that what you share on my Web site may help another parent.

Please stop by my publishing company's Web site. I've listed the site below and plan to keep information you may find useful updated. I produce a monthly newsletter you can subscribe to if you're interested.

Kira Janene Holt

I write fiction for fun. It's darker and meaner than I am in real life. You know, I had to plug my fiction. You can also find information about my fiction on my Web site.

```
www.KiowaHillPublishing.com
```

So now you know how to help your kid ready for college. It's time to head into the college readiness kitchen and start cooking. I hope this cookbook has taken the surprises out of preparing the feast and that your kid is happy and successful with his college choice.

Best of luck to you and your kid!

Hugs,
Kira

Quick List of Guide Web sites

Career Information

www.explorestudent.org
    ACT college readiness assessment for students in grade eight and nine with interest inventory

www.planstudent.org
    ACT college readiness assessment for students in grade ten with interest inventory

http://www.bls.gov/ooh/about/sources-of-career-information.htm

U.S Department of Labor, Bureau of Labor Statistics.

The Occupational Outlook Handbook—online. This government site updates occupations every two years. Extensive listing of different occupations by a variety of search tactics. Available in English and Spanish.

http://www.careeronestop.org/ExploreCareers/SelfAssessments/FindAssessments.aspx

Assessment of interests and abilities. CareerOneStop is sponsored by the U. S. Department of Labor, Employment and Training Administration

Warnings about For-Profit Colleges

http://studentaid.ed.gov/students/attachments/siteresources/ChooseSchoolCarefully.pdf

http://www.bbb.org/us/article/look-for-seven-red-flags-when-applying-to-a-for-profit-college-24540

Searching for Colleges

www.hbcuconnect.com
   Historically black colleges and universities

www.hacu.net
   Hispanic colleges and universities

www.hillel.org
   Jewish student life

www.Knowhow2go.org
   This is the link from the federal government's financial aid site. Besides the college search, this site has links to all kinds of information about college planning.

http://nces.ed.gov/collegenavigator/
National Center for Educational Statistics College Navigator

College Fairs and College Application Fee Waiver Form

www.nacacnet.org
National Association for College Admission Counseling
   This is a great resource for all kinds of good information about the college admission process. They even have a college application fee waiver for students who qualify.

http://www.nacacnet.org/STUDENTINFO
/FEEWAIVER/Pages/default.aspx
   NACAC fee waiver form

College Entrance Exams

http://www.actstudent.org/
   ACT registration

http://student.collegeboard.org
   SAT registration

http://www.learnmoreindiana.org/college
/applying/AdmissionsRequirements/Pages
/ACT_SAT.aspx
   Indiana ACT/SAT Comparison Chart

http://www.act.org/aap/concordance/
   ACT to SAT Conversion Chart

Common Applications

https://www.commonapp.org/CommonApp
/default.aspx
EDU, Inc.

Common Black College Application

http://www.eduinconline.com/
This site allows students to apply to over thirty historically black colleges and universities (HBCU) with one application and for one application fee.

Financial Aid Web Sites

http://www.fafsa.ed.gov
Apply for financial aid here

https://profileonline.collegeboard.com/prf/index.jsp
College Board's CCS Financial Aid Profile
Required by some schools-—fee attached.

http://www.fafsa.ed.gov/deadlines.htm
State deadlines

http://www.pin.ed.gov/PINWebApp/pinindex.jsp
Creating a Personal Identification Number (PIN)

http://studentaid.ed.gov/PORTALSWebApp/students/english/funding.jsp#02

Information about Student Loan Fees and Interest Rates

http://studentaid.ed.gov/students
/publications/student _ guide/index.html
   A free 52-page booklet to download in English or Spanish

http://www.college.gov/wps/portal
   The entry portal to the government financial aid site

Scholarship Information

http://www.ftc.gov/bcp/edu/microsites
/scholarship/
   Stay alert to scholarship scams

http://wdcrobcolp01.ed.gov/Programs/EROD
/org _ list.cfm?category _ ID=SHE

Link to List of State Departments of Higher Education

https://studentaid2.ed.gov/getmoney
/scholarship/v3browse.asp
   This is the federal site for finding scholarships with directions for how to use it.

http://www.collegenet.com/mach25/app
CollegNET

http://www.scholarships.com/
Scholarships.com

http://www.finaid.org/scholarships/
   A large search engine

http://scholarshipamerica.org/open_scholarships.php
Scholarship America
   From there, you can link to other search services.

https://bigfuture.collegeboard.org/scholarship-search
   College Board's scholarship search

Don't forget to visit my Web site to leave comments and suggestions. Sign up for my monthly newsletter.

      http://KiowaHillPublishing.com

About the Author

KIRA JANENE HOLT believes education is the key that unlocks the potential for a bright future. Her professional career and life mission has been to help young people achieve their dreams. She started her career as a middle and high school English teacher in rural Southeast Texas. She left teaching to work at the university level and assisted students in making the transition from high school to college. Additionally she worked at non-profit agencies focused on helping students with psychological and social issues to help ensure their academic success. For the past sixteen years, Kira has been at a not-for-profit research organization that provides solutions to school districts focused on college readiness issues. Kira obtained her Bachelor of Arts degree from Texas State University in English and is certified to teach secondary English and history. She obtained her Master of Arts in Human Services with an emphasis on psychological and social services from St. Edward's University. Kira lives and writes in the hills southwest of Austin, Texas.